KEEP PUSHING FORWARD

Marilyn Wade

A.K.A. MOTHER LOVE

Always remember to:
P—*Pray*
U—*Until*
S—*Something*
H—*Happens*

Stand firm on GOD'S words.

This book is dedicated to my children,
Glenford Wade II and Madalyn Ann Wade.

It is also dedicated to my grandchildren,
Mason Mcallister, Madison Mcallister,
and Asia Wade.

Additional dedications to my siblings,
Melvin, Shirley, James, Donald, Carol, and Leon,
and to my husband, Glenford Wade, Sr.

Contents

KEEP PUSHING FORWARD

Foreword

It says in the Bible, "Give us this day our daily bread."

Remember we have 24 hours in a day. Pick up your cross daily. It doesn't matter if you win or lose that day. Pick up your values again the next day and "keep pushing forward" until the next day comes.

Start to speak the words out of your mouth that you want to happen, such as: "I will," "I did," "I choose to," "It will happen." Speak all words that state it has already happened.

No matter what you endure in life, self-control is strength. You have to get to a point where your mood doesn't shift based on what you're going through, and if it does, make it temporary. Don't allow your emotions to overpower your life.

Don't focus on all the good things until you pray for all the GOD things.

When your self-worth goes up, your net worth goes along with it, as long as you have GOD first.

The colorful heart on my book represents all the people in the world spreading love.

Just *Keep Pushing Forward*. Love always wins.

I am not a prisoner to the situations I go through. I am a survivor.

I am not a product of my environment. I am a child of God.

As long as we look outside of Self—with a capital S—to find out who we are, to define ourselves, and to give us self-worth, we are setting ourselves up to be victims.

I am not a victim—I am a child of God first, then I am a survivor. When we start to look outside ourselves to people, places, things, money, property, and prestige for fulfilment and happiness, it does not work. It is dysfunctional. We cannot fill the hole with anything outside of Self. We must choose the life within us.

You can get all of the money, property, and prestige in the world, have everything, and have everyone adore you. But if you are not at peace within, if you don't love and accept God first, then none of it will make you truly happy.

When we look outside for self-definition and self-worth, we are giving our power away and setting ourselves up for failure.

I am not a failure. I am a survivor.

Acknowledgements

To my mom, Annabell Jefferies, who always told me that anything I believed I could achieve. I believed my mom.

To my children: Glenford W. Wade II and Madalyn Ann Wade, who always thought I was a silly, strange mom, but they always loved and believed in me.

To all those who believe in love, and pushing forward despite what the world thought and how they made you feel. Always believe in yourself.

To the Pontiac Free Library who knew I had no clue on how to get this book started, but then they pushed me in the right direction.

To Steven at Stillwater River Publications. Thank you for taking the time with me to understand me, and to understand what I wanted to tell my children and generations to come.

Introduction

As a child growing up in the projects, we did not have a lot. I was raised by a single mom, because she got divorced. She raised seven children on her own. She was the best mom in the world. She loved the lord, she was a loving, kind, caring hard working woman who always took care of her family first. Even though she had her own struggles, she was always willing to help someone else in need, and this is why I have to write this book, especially about spreading love. When I was a young child I needed a lot of love. So, as I got older I always tried to live a meaningful life every day. I did not always get what I wanted, but she made sure I had what I needed. I had big dreams, and I never gave up on them. I always kept the Faith, and kept pushing forward to accomplish my dreams. My mom always said, even if you cannot see it yet, write your vision, read your vision, and run towards your vision every day. She told me every day that I could be whatever I wanted to be. She said I just can't quit. She said I can be and have all the things I want in life as long as I work hard and keep pushing forward. It is at your reach, it all depends on how bad you want it. Don't let fear stop you, plan it out, and do your research. She said to me as I take this journey called life, things will happen, and try to distract you from what I really wanted to do, and be in life. She told me to not let anything distract me, just stay focused. As you are staying focused, and following your dreams, learn to spread love to others. and put no one before GOD. Always keep him first in your life, in JESUS name AMEN.

1

Beat It, Don't Let It Beat You /
Keep the Faith

While on a cold snowy night, with the moon shining bright, while sleeping in my bed, with sugar plums dancing in my head. I suddenly woke up and was looking out the window, it was a beautiful sight just to watch the snow blow. I noticed a tree, which looked like a bird, that was looking at me. It was shaped like a dove, which I always loved. I decided to get up and go outside.

While walking to the tree, I was just as happy as I could be. To my surprise, and suddenly, I all of a sudden felt some heaviness in my chest. I felt so bad I had to take a rest. I stopped and all of a sudden I felt my body dropping. My hand did reach the end of the tree, but my mind was saying, "What can this be?" I believed I had just fallen to my knees.

The next thing I knew, I was being pushed down a hall. Where the darkness and some light tend to fall. I knew not where I was, but I realized life does what it does. I was not in the same location, I really felt as though I had taken a mini vacation. What happened in a split second, I did not know? It's like my life changed, like when you hear the wind blow. The only thing I really knew was that I needed help for myself, but I did not know what to do. To my surprise, I could not arise, I was on a gurney. I ask myself what was this journey?

2

Your Normal Is Not My Normal / GOD Is in Charge

While just going through what I thought was just a normal day, I did not know how long I was this way. While watching this couple who walked by I could not speak out, but I did not know why, so I began to cry. No words would come out of my mouth, at that time I knew something was wrong with no doubt. I could see, but I could not speak, and my body was feeling very weak. I could move but I could not walk. I could hear but I could not talk. The place had very big windows. I looked through the big windows, I saw the sun and the snow, but how long I was like this I did not know.

All of a sudden I heard my mom's voice. I was so happy I wanted to rejoice, As she got closer and I heard her say: Don't worry my baby, mom is here, I am never too far away. That day is when I learned that our Suddenlies can happen anytime, any hour, or any day. My mom was talking to the doctors, and while they were talking they walked away. I believe they did this because I was only ten and they did not want me to hear what they had to say. After around two weeks the doctors let me go home, but with all this excitement it made my mind roam. While riding home in the car with mom, she was being very quiet, and staying calm. She would normally be laughing, smiling and joking with me, but at this time she was only stirring through the rearview mirror like she was looking through it every second to see and check on me.

3

Love Conquers All

As we drove up to the front of the house, my sisters and brothers greeted me with a loud shout and a big hug and showed me so much love. I could tell that they missed me, as much as I missed them, because I was so glad to see them again. My mom said ok it's time for you to take your medicine and get some rest, because in two days you have to go take some tests. I asked my mom what about school? She said I would not be going back to school for a little while. I asked her why not? She said, don't worry about anything. Everything is going to be alright. She said to me to rest up, because we have to go see the doctors in a couple of days, but she would never completely answer my question? I started to realize that something was extremely wrong, but she did not want to tell me. My mom was that type of strong woman where she would rather keep things to herself than to talk about it to other people. She was a very private person when it came to her family. Sometimes she had me worried, because she would get very quiet, go into her room and shut her door. The next day she would come out of her room just as happy as she wanted to be. I would ask her if she was ok, she would say to me, baby girl stop worrying about me, I am just fine. So go on outside and get some of that sunshine and fresh air. She told me to not go off the stairs, and don't be playing rough. Then she called my sisters and brothers and told them the same thing to not play with me in a rough way. Now I knew something was wrong, because my siblings and I always played rough together with no problem. But, now she is saying things like this. I did not ask her any more questions about what was wrong with me. I just did what she asked me to do. I know she loves me and she was trying to watch out for me and protect me, so I did not ask any more questions. But, I still did not know what was wrong.

4

Our Heart Is Our Main Vessel

As the days would go by, I would constantly hear my mom cry, as I tiptoed to the bathroom late at night. She thought we were all asleep, but not I. I would hear her cry almost every night. My mom was a beautiful woman with a beautiful spirit, she loved GOD, and she prayed all the time. She was not perfect, but she was loved by many. She worked very hard to take care of her family, and she did double shifts at work sometimes. When I was ten years old my heart was literally broken. My mom found out I had a problem with my Aortic Valve in my heart. I did not really understand what it was, but my mom knew. She constantly took me to the doctors to get my heart checked along with constant x-rays, needles and medication, I just went through the process. I was just a child, and all I wanted to do at that age was go home and play with my brothers and sisters and have fun. Prior to whatever was going on with my body, I was very active. I loved to rollerskate, ice skate, play basketball, dance, sing, ride on the swing, and a lot more things. I was just a busy bee and I had a very creative mind. To me, the world was mine because

I was given so many positive words from my mom all my life. I believed the sky was the limit and I believe the words she said until this day. She has gone home to the lord, but what she left here with me were prayers, positive thinking, speaking, and love. These are the things I grabbed, and held on to. As you completely read this book, you will understand what the heart really means to me, and hopefully you will see and use your heart in a different way. The heart will help you to push forward in life. My heart says to me, this book is part one of my life, and this book is a best seller, a play, and a movie. I am not just writing a book to make some money, I am writing this book, because I know that people can relate to it, and probably have gone through situations of their own. If you are still breathing, your story is still being written every second of your day. I am thankful to have one life with two hearts, But I am very thankful to have a second chance at life.

I write this book to give and to show the next generations how to give. A portion of the proceeds of this book will go to these four charities: the American Heart Association, the American Diabetes Association, the National Kidney Association, and the American Cancer Society.

5

Momma Said Never Stop Dreaming

My oldest sister Shirley Jefferies watched all the younger children while my mom worked. We would all help out in the cleaning, and cooking. We all had to eat our dinner, do our homework, take our baths, put on our pajamas, and then we could relax and watch television for a little while. My favorite shows were musicals like the Jackson Five cartoon show, Grammy Awards, and the Jetsons. I loved music at a very young age. I used to sing in the children's church choir. I also loved to joke, laugh, and play all types of sports, such as basketball, ice skating, singing, dancing, tennis, volleyball, and just being creative and doing other things I thought I could not do. I had a big imagination, and big dreams. At my young age I believed the sky was the limit for what I could do in my life, because my mom said I could do it. My mom would ask me almost every day what I was going to do to get closer to reaching my dream. I said to her, today I want to sing a song to all of you. My sisters and brothers would just laugh at me, but then my mom would tell them they had to listen, after they did their homework, had dinner, and had their baths. I was nervous, because I knew they were going to make jokes.

I used to tell my sister and brothers I was going to be on or go to the Grammy Awards one day. They always laughed at me and said who do you think you are? I told them mommy said I can be and do anything I want in life. I believed my mom. My mom would tell them that I was going to do big things in life, because I have a big imagination, and I was a go-getter. When my mom heard them teasing me she would say leave her alone, because at that time I was the baby. My mom was a single parent, but she took good care of her children, and she helped other people also, who needed help with food, clothing, shelter or anything else they needed. She had a heart of gold. Her name was Annabelle Jefferies.

6

Life Happens Without a Warning

As time went along, maybe around close to a month, my mom said she needed to talk to all of us about something. I asked her, "Mom, what is wrong?" She still would not answer me. She said she was waiting for my sisters and brothers to come down stairs. There were six of us children and she only wanted to say things once, that is why she gathered us up all together. We were all looking at each other wondering what our mom had to tell us. We were all nervous. We thought we had done something wrong.

After everybody sat down at the kitchen table she told me and them that I had to have a major surgery with my heart. That is why I passed out the other day. I have a heart murmur, and in order to fix it I had to have this surgery. It is called: (Open Heart Surgery). She told me if I did not get the surgery, my heart valve would not work properly. She told me that is why I have been taking the medicine. The doctors want to see if this will correct the problem. She said that is why I can not go to school, because it would be too strenuous for me. She said if it did not correct the problem, I would have to have the surgery to live. We all cried together that day. My mom prayed over me many times but, at this time she had my sisters and brothers pray for me. She called her friends, church members, and everybody she could reach to pray for me. I knew within my heart that everything was going to be alright. She always told me that I was GOD'S child. I believed the words she told me, and I really did not know how serious the surgery was going to be. I just looked at it as something that had to be done for me to help me stay healthy. When you are a child you don't really understand the things that adults have to go through. Sometimes we don't understand why they say no when we think it is an ok thing to do. So I just did what my mom wanted me to do.

7

Family and Sibling Love

My sisters and brothers started to cry, because they did not want anything bad to happen to me. I started crying because I was very nervous about having surgery. I now understand why my mom was crying almost every night. She was trying to stay strong by keeping all this news to herself. I was so shocked once I heard that news. She said to all of us, I know this is a lot to take in, so I want all of you to get together and talk and pray. It hit all of us hard, but I believe it hit my oldest sister Shirley the hardest, because she took me as her little baby while mom was working to provide us with food, clothing and shelter. Even after my mom told us this, she still had to go to work. My sisters and brothers asked me if I was nervous, I said yes of course, because I don't know what is going to happen to me. But one thing I do know is that my life was in GOD's hands. I know regardless of what comes my way, if it is better or worse, I am going to be ok. I have my loving family with so much love for me, and I know GOD is going to give me his best. Sometimes families have differences, but you still have to love them, near or far. Because the good lord did not pick and choose if he wanted to love us, so how are we going to pick and choose our neighbor? I just want to spread the love to all people, no matter whatever the race, creed, or color. I believe everybody has good in them and they just have to find it and spread it.

8

Handling Life's Journey Challenges

My mom would constantly talk to the doctors who were supposed to be doing the surgery on the telephone. She probably spoke to them constantly for around a month. But, my mom was also working on getting a second opinion from other doctors before she would give the final approval for them to do the surgery. She did try to explain to me what was going to happen if I did have the surgery, but a lot of it I did not understand, because I was only ten years old. I told my mom, I trust you will make the best decision for me. All she kept saying to me was baby everything will be alright, no matter what we have to do. God has you, and you will be favored. Sometimes when she would say certain things I would not understand what she meant.

9

My Family's Belief in GOD

She said, you trust in GOD first, and always remember you have a praying mom. I believe she was trying to be strong for me, so I would not be afraid. As young children, my mom would make a point to make sure we went to church on Sundays. She would make sure we had our clothes laid out on Saturday night, along with taking our baths, so we had no excuse not to go to church on Sunday. She would wake us up early, make sure we had breakfast, brushed our teeth, combed out hair and had our clothes on before she would leave out the door to go to work. We lived in the projects, where they did not have a lot of transportation.

We had a yellow school bus that came around 8:00am in the morning to take us to church. The driver's name was Buddy George. He was a very nice guy. Sometimes we did not have our bibles, and he would give us one. he kept extras on hand. He was a believer of GOD. All we wanted to do was get together with each other and have fun, because we did not really get to see each other through the week. We would sing songs on the bus like: (He's got the whole world in his hand). and have a lot of fun on the bus with our friends. I always loved to sing.

10

The Hardest Things in Life
Are the Best Rewards

We had a lot of chores through the week, and a lot of studying. My mom was very strict about us getting a good education, because she said she did not want us to have to struggle like she and her parents had to. She said she wanted us to have a better life. But she always told us, no matter what we do in life to always put GOD first, and do our best. If it is college, a trade school or a job.

Even though we grew up in the projects, we had a lot of love, we lived in a community that watched over each other and also would tell your parents if you did something wrong. We had a playground, where the swing was a car tire and a rope. We had a basketball court, which was also a skating rink in the winter. I asked my mom to buy me some ice skates. She said, girl, where am I going to get money for ice skates? I have to use this money for food.

She really said no, but she asked me one day, "Marilyn, would you go outside and get that food out of the car please?" I did and I saw some ice skates in the car that was my size. I was so happy, I gave her a big hug and squeezed her and said thank you mom. Every winter when the ice would fill up in the basketball court and freeze up I was out there skating. People would look at me like I was crazy, but I was not. I just liked to try to do different things. All this happened before I suddenly got sick.

All the apartments at the projects looked the same inside and out. One day we decided to ask our mom if we could do something different outside the front of the house, because we wanted our outside yard to look different. She asked us what do you want to do? We said we only want to plant a small garden with tomatoes, cucumbers, string beans, potatoes, carrots, corn and sunflowers. Her reaction was that she did not know if they would grow. Then she said go ahead and show me what you all can do. She did not think there was enough dirt in our area to do this. She asked us, "Where are you going to get the seeds?" We said we would dry out some of the seeds from the food we ate. She had to buy the sunflower seeds for us, because we did not have any.

11

Marilyn's Special Love Garden

While I was bending over to dig up some dirt, I got a sharp pain in my chest and I let out a scream. My mom ran outside to see what had happened, my sisters and brothers said we don't know what happened to her. Everybody was scared, and stopped digging and planting. Mom told me I had to come in the house and rest. She said I was doing too much. She said she was going to call the doctors to tell them what happened, and ask them what she should do for me.

She called and left a message on their telephone and they called back in around five minutes. The doctor told her to have me rest, and do not do anything strenuous. The doctor asked my mom was I still taking the medicine they prescribed for me? She said yes, and on a daily basis. I have been giving it to her the way it says on the prescription bottle, The doctor said to my mom if I was still having a problem take me to the hospital. I took my medicine, ate some food and went to sleep. Thank GOD everything calmed down as I fell asleep. When I woke up it was the next day and I was feeling much better.

My mom said that the next day I could not help with the completion of planting the garden. She said all I could do was sit in a chair in the yard and watch, but that was ok, at least I had a chance to watch my sisters and brothers finish planting the garden. They said, "Marilyn, this garden is dedicated to you, because we love you so much." They said it is called (Marilyn's Love Garden). I laughed, but I really thought that was very nice, Then I started to cry. They knew I was going through a lot, and I was scared, so they did whatever they could to make me feel better. Every day they would work on the garden and let me watch them. I watched them take care of it as it grew. At first I only saw the flowers starting to bloom.

12

Forgive, Forget, and Give

It took around a month for the vegetables to really start growing on the vines. First the small green tomatoes came, then the string beans, then the cucumbers, then the potatoes, they grew under the ground, then the corn, because it was hard to grow corn in the projects, but we did, they were little corn, but they grew. Last but not least, then the sunflowers. They were very bright and yellow. Everything looked so tasty, and pretty. I was so proud of all my sisters and brothers for the work that they did in the garden. It made me happy and excited every time I watched the vegetables get bigger and bigger.

After around three months, the vegetables were almost ready to be picked. We waited for one more week before we picked them. After that week, we were all excited to go outside to pick our fresh vegetables. But, when we opened the door to go outside to pick our vegetables, we were surprised to see that somebody had already picked almost all of our vegetables that we worked hard to plant. Everybody was in total shock. Me, my sisters, and brothers were so upset we started to cry.

We called our mom outside and we showed her what somebody did. She knew we were upset, and she said don't cry, maybe it was someone who really needed the food more than we did. Think of it as a blessing to someone who really needed it more than us. My mom was always a giver, and she was always helping everybody. She had a heart of gold. The people always would say let's go over Annabell's house. That was my mom's name. They said you know she can cook, she is a southern girl. My mom was born in Raleigh North Carolina and she definitely could cook. She loved to cook. I believe I received her cooking skills, personality, energy and love for others from her. I loved the way she was with people, but if something was not right she would definitely let you know.

13

Divorced Parents Who Still Provide for Their Families

My mom has been a divorced woman for a while, and she was more focused on taking care of her children. One day when she came home she told us she met this nice guy and his name was Mr. Al. She was speaking with him for a little while, and she said she wanted us to meet him. We were a little hesitant about it, because it had only been my mom and us for a long time. But we could see she wasn't always happy, and when she spoke about him she would have a big smile on her face. It was like he was what she was missing in her life. So we all agreed to meet him, because we wanted our mom to be happy, and have someone in her life that she could talk to besides us. We kids had each other to talk too. But, she did not have an adult to talk to. Remember you never stop being a parent, no matter what age the children are.

14

My Mom Met Mr. Al, a Pastor's Son

Mr. Al came over to the house and had dinner with all of us. My mom made all of us put on our Sunday best clothes, so we would look presentable. We could tell he was nervous, and so were we. My mom tried to get him to open up and talk, but it took some time, but finally he started talking. He first started telling us about himself. He said he was a pastor's son, and he had three sisters. I believe he said he was from Arkansas. He said that is where the rest of his family lived. He said he was in the military, and that is how he met our mom.

Then he started to ask us what grades we were in at school, and we told him. Then he asked us what we wanted to be when we grew up and finished school. I said I wanted to be a doctor first, and a singer. I wanted to be like the Jackson Five, and go to the Grammy Awards. Then my sisters and brothers started picking on me again when I said that. He then said, "You can be whatever you want to be. You just have to work hard to get there. But always put GOD first in your life." I knew that because my mom always told us that.

As we started to see Mr. Al more and more with our mom we felt a little more comfortable with him. He started to treat all of us as though we were his children. We asked him if he had any children, and he said no, but as time went along, we felt as though we were his children. We knew we were not, but we had fun with him. He would show us how to do our chores better, and quicker, and help us with our homework, so we could have a little more fun time. But, he was the same way my mom was when it came to getting our education, and studying.

15

My Mom and Mr. Al
Both Believed in Education

He told us that he was in college, and he was going to school to get his master's degree. I looked at him and said, but you are old. He looked at us children and said you are never too old to keep getting your education. There is always something new to learn. He said life changes every day. At that point and time, from what I had just experienced, I definitely believed what he was saying, as things change every day. I did not know if he knew what I was going through, but I did not say anything about it. Mr. Al used to always sit down and talk to us about education. He was an older person, but he was still going to college. I asked him didn't you already finish high school? He said yes, I finished it a long time ago. Mr. Al was also in a uniform sometimes when he came over to see my mom. I asked my mom why he was in a uniform. She told me he was in the navy. So, I asked Mr. Al why are you still studying classes for school. He said I am in college now. I did not know too much about college, because I had a long way to go before I got there. He said he went to one college for two years and he received his Associates Degree, and he went to college for two more years and he received his Bachelor's Degree. He said now he was going for his PHD. I said to him that is a lot of schooling. He said to me education was the key to success along with hard work.

16

Sickness Will Attack You Out of Nowhere

As the days went by, I started to not feel the best. My mom had gone to work that morning, everybody was still sleeping, because they did not have to get up until 6:00am. Mr. Al would come over in the morning to make sure we made it off to school on time. He walked in the house, and he heard someone moaning. It was me, I had those bad pains in my chest again. He asked me if I was alright, I said no. I don't feel good. My chest hurts.

He woke my sisters and brothers up and asked them if they knew what was wrong with me. Nobody answered. He called my mom and told her something was wrong with me. My mom told him she would be right there, she was leaving work right now. This was on a Friday. My mom called the doctors and told them I was having problems breathing. The doctors said to call the ambulance and they would meet her at the hospital. Mr. Al watched the rest of my sisters and brothers while I went to the hospital in the ambulance. They were very nervous and crying. My mom told them don't worry, I was going to be alright.

17

Doctors Doing Their Job

When I got to the hospital they took me right in, hooked me up to the heart monitor, and put some needles in my arms and had some bags hanging over me. I was in the emergency room. When my mom arrived, they asked her if she was my mother, she said yes. She asked them if I was going to be ok. They told her we are waiting for the doctors to come, they are on their way. We are going to keep a watch on her until they get here.

When the doctors got there they examined me and then brought me to a hospital room. I believe they gave me something for the pain and to go to sleep, because when I woke up, I was in another room. I noticed there was another girl in the room with me. I said hello, my name is Marilyn. I asked her what her name was and she said her name was Lisa. I asked her why she was in the hospital. She said because she had something wrong with her heart, and she had to have surgery at 4:00am in the morning. As she was telling me this some people walked in the room and tried to shoosh her, and tell her to stop talking. I believe it was her mom and dad.

My mom was out of the room also while we were

talking. I could tell my mom was very nervous and had been crying. The doctors called my mom out of the room, because they wanted to talk to her. She said to me baby I will be right back, I have to talk to the doctors. Here is your buzzer to call the nurse if you need them. It was a little while before my mom came back to my room. She had this sad look on her face when she came back in. She said baby girl, I have to tell you something. She said the doctors said that the medicine they were giving you was not working and I had no choice but to have you have the surgery. She and I cried together because we both knew already there was a possibility that the medicine would not work.

18

This Surgery Had to Happen

My mom told me all about this beforehand, that this could happen, what little I could understand when she was telling me. I said, "Mom, I am ok having the surgery." My mom told me she loved me and she did not want me to go through this trauma all my life, not knowing when I was going to get chest pains, get sick, or something worse. She said I want you to have somewhat of a normal life like the other children. I told her I trust God and I trust you mom, so let's get this done.

My mom went back to the doctors to sign all the paperwork that needed to be signed for the surgery. She came back to me and told me I would have the surgery on Monday morning at 4:00am. I thought, this is the same time my new friend Lisa was going down stairs to have her surgery, but her surgery was on a Saturday. Lisa and I talked a lot to each other about what we like to do, our siblings, our parents, and what we wanted to be when we grow up. It was fun talking to a person that could understand what I was going through, and dealing with.

19

Lisa Understood What I Was Going Through

As time went along the morning came for Lisa to be prepared to have her surgery. I woke up, because there were so many people in the room talking to her and preparing her for surgery. I did not see anything they were doing because they shut the curtains. But, I did see her mom and dad walk in the room. They told her that they loved her and mommy and daddy will be right here when you come out of the surgery. Then I heard them give her a kiss. The doctors started to wheel her out of the room in her bed. I had to say something to her before she went to surgery. I told her I will see you when you come back upstairs. She said ok. Everybody was surprised I was awake.

I finally went back to sleep for the rest of the night. I knew it was the next day when I opened my eyes and I saw the sun shining bright through the windows. My mom was sleeping in the lounge chair next to me. I did not wake her up, because I knew she was tired. I had to say something to see if my friend Lisa was back from her surgery. I said good morning Lisa, she said with a faint voice good morning. I did not want to say too much to her because I knew she had just gone through a major surgery. All I could see was the nurses coming in and out of her bed area. They still had her curtains closed where I could not see her at all, but I was glad I heard her voice.

I am not sure, but I believe her mom and dad stayed overnight at the hospital until the surgery was over. When they came in to see her they had the same clothes on that they had on the day before. They said good morning to me, then went to spend time with their daughter. They looked like they had not slept all night. They looked very tired, and like they needed some rest.

My mom woke up and went home for a minute to shower, change her clothes, check on my sisters and brothers, and make sure everything was ok at the house. She was also constantly calling them while she was at the hospital with me. She would talk to Mr. Al and thank him for staying at the house with my other sister and brothers, and making sure they did what they needed to do, which were go to school, keep the house clean, eat, take a bath, do homework, and study.

He was a very good man to my mom and all of us. He would always call my mom Annabelly. That was his nickname he had for her. He would say, "Annabelly, I am here to help you and your family whenever you need me."

That made my mom very happy, because most of the time she was doing everything on her own with her children's help. Now she knew she had someone who was there for her and her children. My mom was a very proud and strong woman.

When my mom got back to the hospital she would give me a hug and a big kiss and tell me she loved me. She would sit down in the comfortable lounge chair beside my bed and watch television with me.

20

Lisa's Mom and Dad
Went Home to Change

Lisa parents wanted to go home and shower and change their clothes, so Lisa's mom and my mom started talking to each other, and then Lisa's mom and my mom exchanged numbers, because they both wanted to keep in touch with each other about how the both of us were doing, and allow us to talk to each other. Lisa's mom said my husband and I want to go home and take a shower and change clothes. They asked my mom if she could keep an eye on Lisa. They said they would not be long. She said yes and they said thank you. Then they kissed Lisa, told her they loved her and walked out the door.

While my mom and I were watching television, we heard some noise at Lisa's bed. It sounded like she was having a problem breathing. All of a sudden I heard the words code blue, I will never forget those words. A lot of doctors and nurses ran in the room to the bed where Lisa was so quick with all this machinery, I was so scared, I did not know what was happening. My mom called Lisa's mom and told her and her husband to come back, because something was happening to Lisa.

21

Experiencing a Traumatic Situation Before My Surgery

My mom told me to calm down because she saw me getting nervous. My mom was afraid for me so she asked some of the nurses to take me out of the room, and put me in another room, and they did. They were doing something to Lisa, but I did not know what it was. All of a sudden Lisa's mom and dad made it back to the hospital. They were frantic, because they were not gone that long, and they did not even make it into their house.

They were asking questions to the doctors and asking the doctors what happened. They told the parents, we will tell you as we go back to the operating room, she is bleeding profusely. So the parents followed them while they rushed Lisa back to the operating room. After they took her I was afraid that what just happened to her might happen to me when I go down for my surgery on Monday morning. Remember I am only ten years and I just experienced another trauma from a friend I just met.

22

This Is When I Realized Love Has No Color

The doctors had to come in and give me something to make me calm down, and go to sleep, because they did not want me to be a nervous wreck before I went down to have the same surgery. By the time I woke up it was night time. My mom asked me if I was alright. I said yes, then I asked her if Lisa had come back in the room yet. My mom said no. I said I hope my friend Lisa is ok. My mom was exhausted. They had to give her something also, to relax her nerves until it was my time to get prepared for my surgery the next morning at 4:00am.

23

Now My Time for My Surgery

As the time went along it was getting closer to the time for me to go down to surgery. I took another nap and when I woke up again they were standing over me preparing me for my surgery. They woke my mom up also to let her know it was time for the surgery. It was dark out. I asked them what time it was. They said it was 4:00 Monday morning. They did whatever they had to do to prepare me for the surgery. My mom was praying over me and with me before I went down. My mom told me she loved me and gave me a big hug and a kiss and said to me you are in GOD'S hands, and you are going to be alright. She asked the surgeons if she could pray over them before the surgery. they said yes, so she did. Then she walked with the surgeons and me down to the operating room. My mom said I will be right here when you come out of surgery. Before I went in she said I love you baby. I told her I love you too mom.

My mom asked the doctors how long the surgery will take. The doctor told her it would take around six hours. As the doctors wheeled me into the operating room, all I could see was a whole lot of bright lights, doctors, metal equipment, pans, and pointy objects. The doctor then put a mask over my mouth and nose and told me to keep taking some deep breaths. I did that probably around three times, and I did not know anything else after that. until I got out of surgery, and then the recovery room.

24

My Mom Would Not Leave the Hospital

I was told, after the surgery, that at the time of the surgery my mom was walking the floors and would not go home. They said the doctor told her she looked exhausted and should go home and get some rest, because I would be in surgery for quite a while, and then the recovery room. But, my mom said no she was not going to be leaving the hospital. Then the doctor said to one of the nurses, please find Mrs. Jefferies a hospital room for the night to stay here. So, my mom had somebody bring her a change of clothing to the hospital. She took a shower and laid down in bed. Before she knew it she was knocked out. I guess the doctor was right, she was exhausted, because in reality she was awake for around a day with no food, she was only drinking cups of coffee.

As my mom was sleeping, she heard someone calling her name and tapping her shoulder. It was the doctor coming to tell her that the surgery went well, and I was in the recovery room. My mom asked the doctor how long I would be there. They told her around three hours. The first words that came out of my mom's mouth was,

"Thank you Jesus to GOD be the glory. Carry these words with you at all times, keep praying and always have a relationship with GOD." She was up now, just thanking GOD. She finally got an appetite to eat, so she went downstairs in the cafeteria room where they had food for the visitors and she got herself a coffee and a donut.

25

The Good News

My mom was so happy she called the rest of the family, she talked to Mr. Al and told him the good news, and he said thank GOD. My mom asked him to put Shirley on the phone and she told her to tell my sister and brothers I was ok. She told them that I got through the surgery alright and I am doing fine. She told them I was in the recovery room now, and I would be in there for a while, because the doctors had to keep an eye on me to make sure there were no problems. My mom was so excited she could not wait until I got in my hospital room.

Around three hours later they told my mom I was in the regular room in the hospital. My mom was so excited that she stopped eating when they said I was in a room and came up to see me. When she walked in the room she was in shock, because she did not expect to see so many tubes, bags, and machines on my body. She was so shocked she had to turn around and walk out the room to cry and get herself together. She came back in and gave me a kiss on my forehead and told me she loved me. I was not really awake. I was dozing in and out of sleep. I was exhausted.

The doctor told my mom I would probably sleep for the rest of the day and night. He told her I was exhausted from the surgery, and what my body just went through. He told her I needed to get some rest. But, my mom would not leave my bedside. She stayed there, prayed over me and just waited for me to wake up. As she was watching television she fell asleep in the lounge chair that they provided for her to sleep in. We both did not wake up until the next day.

26

The Day I Finally Fully Woke Up

On the next day when I woke up my body was in so much pain. The nurses had to come into the room and give me more pain medicine. My mom heard the nurses in my room and she asked them how I was doing. The nurse told her she is doing alright. the nurse said, "You both had a good night's sleep, which you both needed." She told my mom the doctor will be in this morning to check on me, but she did not know what time the doctors were coming. So we just sat and kept trying to talk in between my nodding out on her.

As time went along, the nurses were in and out of my hospital room checking my heart, blood pressure, temperature, stool and many other things. These are the only things that I knew what they were checking. There were so many bags hanging and so many machines attached to me, that it made me a little nervous. But I just stayed calm and did what the nurses wanted me to do.

27

The Healing Process

I was getting a little better every day. At least that is what the doctor was telling my mom. Every day they had to change the bags that I had on me. I believe the tube that was in my throat they took out on the third day, and that was when I could talk to my mom again. My mom was so glad they took it out so she could talk to me, and I could talk to her a little. On the fourth day they gave me some broth to drink, because my throat was still sore, and I really could not swallow yet. I had to drink that for around a week.

All my vital signs were good, and my progress of healing was going well. As I was getting better I asked my mom if she had heard anything about Lisa. She would not answer me, she would always change the subject and tell me Marilyn you have to focus on your healing so you can go home. I said yes mom I will. I believe it was the second week when they started to give me soft solid foods, and at that time I was hungry and getting an appetite. I would eat my food and ask them if I could have some more. They would say we cannot give you a lot because your body has gone through a traumatic change. I then would ask for some juice or water. They said I could have all of that I wanted.

They gradually started taking me off of the machines one at a time. Every day I was feeling a little better. As time rolled along, they finally let me eat some solid foods. This was around the third week. They then told my mom I might be able to go home the following week, because I was doing well and my surgery was healing properly. I was told they had to replace my Aortic Valve which is attached to my heart. I was getting very excited because pretty soon I would be able to go home to see my sisters and brothers. I was missing them a lot.

28

Finally, It's Time to Go Home

The following week came, and the doctors released me to go home. They gave my mother paperwork on the do's and don'ts for me, and some prescription medicine to take. There were a lot of things that I could not do for a while which was running around, I still had to stay out of school for two months, I could not lift heavy objects, I could not do strenuous exercises or activities, and I had to keep myself calm. I had to eat differently. It was like I was just there. But, I was thankful that I was still here. So once my mother told me all these things, I listened.

Once they said I could go home, I kept asking my mom can we go now? She told me to calm down, she said I was getting too excited. The nurses, and my mom bathe me, and help me put my clothes on to get ready to go. Before they walked me out of the hospital in the wheelchair they took my vital signs again to make sure everything was still ok. I was at this hospital for quite a while, and the staff was so good to me. I could not leave without saying thank you to all of them. I was going to miss them, but I missed my family more.

29

Thank You God for Bringing My Mom's Spirit Back

They helped me in the car and I was so happy because I was on my way home. The entire outside looked so different, because I had not been out for four weeks. I just sat in the back seat of my mom's car while she was driving. My mom started joking and laughing with me this time while we're riding. I said to myself, now this is the mom I know, she is coming back to herself. As we got closer to the house I saw some sunflowers, vegetables, neighbors, balloons and I heard my favorite Jackson Five song "Ben". I felt that way because I believed people did not understand me. When I got out of the car my sister and brothers gave me an easy hug so they would not hurt me. I was so glad to see that my sisters and brothers planted "Marilyn's Love Garden" again.

I gave it around a month and then I asked my mom about Lisa again, she sat down. I have something to tell you. That day when they took Lisa back down stairs to the operating room again they could not save her. She did not make it, she passed away. She was bleeding internally and the doctors could not stop it. My mom said she did not want to tell me because she believed it was going to affect me before I had my surgery. She was Caucasian and I am black, and I made it. This tells me color does not matter. We are all human beings. No, it is not right the way some of us are treated in this world, but I am going to try to spread the love as much as I can, as long as I have breath in my body.

30

The Heart Does Matter

At a very young age, I learned that the heart does matter, literally, and life itself is made of a lot of suddenlies. I don't sweat the small stuff, and even the big stuff I don't claim. I know life is going to happen, no matter what. No matter what I go through in life, I just say I am here to experience this journey called life. The doctors told my mom they had to bring me back, because they almost lost me, and I say thank you GOD. We just have to believe in GOD and keep pushing forward, so he can get us to where he wants us to be, so he can get the glory. I realized that a trip through my pass brings me closer to my future. A lot of people really did not understand me, and why I was the way I was, caring, loving, giving, a dreamer and believer, and that is why I spread love as much as I can. GOD knows my heart and he doesn't make any mistakes. Nobody can ever tell your story better than you can. This is my testimony, and nobody can tell it better than me.

31

Mother Love It Says / Keep Spreading the Love

P.S. Everybody always puts GOD first. Keep loving, living, laughing, praying, believing, and forgiving. Always keep hope, faith and giving. Keep your joy, peace and happiness. I love you all, but GOD loves you more. Everybody have a blessed day and keep spreading the love.

YOU GOT THIS

This is the introduction on why we must love more
We never know what another person is going through
Love People, Spread Love, Like Things.
Believe and Receive whatever GOD has for you
Life's situations will happen out of nowhere.
Who are you going to believe, GOD's word,
    or the world's word.
Make room for a more meaningful and enjoyable life
Stuff is not real it doesn't matter, because you can't
    take it with you
GOD'S design is bigger and larger than we could
    ever imagine
What we do in life, GOD allows us to do.
Ask yourself, what is your definition of spreading love?
Ask yourself, what distractions are stopping you from
    doing something meaningful?
Ask yourself, what can you change to improve your
    values in life?
Ask yourself, when have you felt your most alive inside?

Yes, I was blessed to heal my heart, body, mind, and soul, and I thank GOD that all my dreams came true.

After the surgery and when I went to high school I was able to play sports, which were, basketball, volleyball, running track, tennis, and more. I was also blessed to play instruments which were piano, violin, and trumpet. I also wrote music, and did videos of my music, which all are copyrights in the Congress of Washington. After high school I went to college, and trade schools. I did not take courses for what I loved, I had to take courses to earn money to pay my bills. But I still never gave up on my music. I did that part-time and on the weekends at Oakland Beach in Warwick, RI, I opened the basketball game singing the National Anthem for the PC Friars. I played baseball with Michael Bolton and his band in Warwick RI. I also sang the National Anthem at the oldest baseball league in Pawtucket. I sang at the Chateau Deville, Warwick, RI, the Pelham House nightclub in Providence, I performed at Dunkin Donuts Center, with the Carolyn Dutra Dancers. I put a choir together to perform for the Bridal Show.

At this time I was working for a mortgage company. There was a person who knew how much I loved, and wanted to be involved in any aspect of the music industry, and they told me WPRO Radio station was looking for someone to be a traffic Manager. I knew nothing about it, but my heart was telling me to take a leap of faith. I took the time to read up about it, I went to my interview, and I got the job. I was so excited that my dream came true. I loved it. I felt like I was where I was supposed to be. It took some time to get there, but I was so thankful I finally got there.

The next surprise I received, I noticed a person in there with me who I knew who he was from seeing him on television. His name was Salty Brine. I was so shocked to see him. He was a celebrity to me. He was so nice to me, he came over to me and introduced himself, and welcomed me to the radio station. I said thank you very much. Then, I was introduced to everyone in the building. Then I was given my keys to get in the building. I met a lot of the on air personalities, like Tony Bristol, Rocky Allen, Milt Fullerton, Maryann Sorentino, Big John Bina, TJ Napp, and more. It was such a beautiful experience for me on that day.

When the celebrities came to the radio station to promote their songs on the radio, they would take pictures with us, and give autographs once they were finished doing their on air promotion with the DJ. You can see the photos on my Facebook—Marilyn Wade.

Now, it has been around a year that I was working at WPRO Radio station, and DJ Milt Fullerton told me he wanted me to bring some of my music that I wrote, because he wanted to see and hear it, so I did. I did not ask any questions, I just did it. The next day he was on air, and he asked someone to come and get me from my office because he wanted to do an interview with me and put my music on the air. When he started introducing me, he said, "Yes, we are at the Radio Station, and I found out we have great talent right here at the station working with us right down the hall and her name is Marilyn Wade."

The biggest surprise of my life was when I went into work one morning, and I noticed an envelope on my desk. I thought it was some paperwork I needed to do for my day of work. But to my surprise, it brought me to tears. At that moment I was so emotional, I could not speak. I shut my office door and cried for a moment. Someone gave me two Grammy Award tickets and hotel accommodations I only had to pay for the plane ticket. I left my office and asked everybody who gave me these tickets, I want to thank them. I finally went to the program directors office. Her name was Karen, she had such a big smile on her face. She said Marilyn I gave you those tickets. She said I wanted to make your dream come true. She said all I want you to do is report back to us on how the Grammy Awards was. I said yes I will do that.

This is why I say, dreams do come true, we don't know how, when, where, or why. This is what I want to leave back here with my children, grandchildren, and extended generations and the ones who are not born yet. Always keep GOD first, and always pray. Recently, I performed at the Apollo Theatre, I performed on the show the VOICE, and I performed for America's Got Talent All things happen on GODS timing. Keep your

Faith. If you Believe It, you can Receive It, and Achieve It. Never give up on what you want to do. I am now sixty two, and I still have a lot more to do. You are beautiful and wonderfully made in GOD'S image. No matter what situations you have to go through in life you are perfectly made. Nanna is going to leave you with generational wealth, and health with the words that I am leaving in my book, for you, to start your first short story of your own books, and the best person you can wake up and speak to, which is the all-mighty GOD. My grandbabies, as long as you are not hurting nobody or harming nobody to do what you want to do in life, or be who you want to be in life just go for it. If you do it this way you will have no guilt in whatever you go out to accomplish in your life. Every night when you lay your head down to sleep you will sleep in peace. Don't do what others do to you, do what you think is right. I want my children, grandbabies, and generations to come to **KEEP PUSHING FORWARD.** Prayers have been left here for you to accomplish anything you want in life Just plant the seeds as tiny as a mustard seed. Carry these with you at all times: Father/GOD, Son/Jesus, and the Holy Spirit. Keep praying, Have a relationship with GOD, spread love, positivity, Hope, Peace, Joy and Happiness wherever you go. Plant seeds, Forgive, Give and keep the Faith.

Nanna's Grandbabies' Life Journey

By Marilyn Wade, A.K.A "Mother Love"

Mother Love says…
"I will always pray for you,
Mason, Madison, and Asia.
I will pray and love you for eternity."

Nanna's Words to You

Always remember Mason, Madison and Asia the prayers I prayed for you are still working for you, even when I am not here. Start your day with prayer and speaking to God. Keep GOD in your life first in all things that you do. God will never leave you or forsake you. Always trust in him, and always thank him even when times get rough. Just call on God, and always keep your faith not fear. Because, no matter what you're going through, GOD will take care of you. Always thank him for all things and give him the glory. Always pray everything in Jesus name. AMEN after you pray. Always have a relationship with GOD, and spend time with him every day. Always go to GOD first whenever you are going through things in your life, because you will always go through this journey called life. Then, if you need to speak to others, do that. Always remember Nanna will always love you infinitely and beyond, even if I am not here in body, I am here in spirit. Remember every day I am telling you I love you, and whatever you want to be, or do in life, you can. Always keep GOD first. He will help you to reach your goals. If he brings you to it, he will get you through it. You can do all things, just never give up. Always be ready to fight one more round, because that is what makes a champion. Tell your mom, my beautiful daughter, Madalyn that I am proud of her as a parent, and everything I am saying to you in this book, I am also saying to Madalyn/daughter and Glenford/son I want you all to do what you love, but also use the knowledge I left here with you.

As Mother Love Always Says...

The words of the day are:
Love life to the fullest.
Live life in the moment.
Laugh each and every day.

MASON

YOU GOT THIS

Write a book about what you love:

SOCCER

To: _Mason_

From: _Nanna with love_

Date: _February 2022_

Now start your book.

MADISON

YOU GOT THIS

Write a book about what you love:

GYMNASTICS

To: _____ *Madison*

From: _____ *Nanna with love*

Date: _____ *February 2022*

Now start your book.

ASIA

YOU GOT THIS

Write a book about what you love:

BALLET

To: _____ *Asia*

From: _____ *Nanna with love*

Date: _____ *February 2022*

Now start your book.

I want to leave these words with the generations that will come after me and others. Everybody has a past, as you live your life you will create a pass. The only thing wrong with the past is that we don't want to leave it in the past. Whatever you do in life you normally have to deal with the consequences of your actions, but you can only live in the now, and we do not know what the future holds.

You can only live in the now, because we don't know what tomorrow will bring. We can't predict the future. Every day, live your life as though it was the end of your life. Make the rest of your life be the best of your life. Spread the love each and every day, because we never know what another person is going through. This is why I love so hard, because I got my second chance.

About the Author

The reason why I decided to write this first book is because I got a second chance at the age of ten. Also, because of this pandemic, and the history that we lost. I am also speaking to their children, my children, their grandbabies, and my grandbabies. I wanted to leave this book with my children, and generations after them. I did not want to leave this earth without them truly knowing me starting from childhood. Hopefully God will keep me here to complete the books for as long as I can. I am now sixty-two years old.

I want to inspire people to never give up on their life or their dreams, no matter what situation life hands to them.

Made in the USA
Middletown, DE
26 April 2024

53473998R00046